The Secure Retirement Method for Members of The Florida Retirement System

HOW TO COORDINATE YOUR FRS RETIREMENT
BENEFITS, SOCIAL SECURITY, MEDICARE AND
OTHER SAVINGS TO CREATE YOUR OWN
SECURE RETIREMENT PLAN

John H. Curry

JOHNHCURRY.COM

John H Curry, CLU®, ChFC®, AEP, MSFS®, CLTC, Registered Representative and Financial Advisor of Park Avenue Securities LLC (PAS). Securities products and advisory services offered through PAS, member FINRA, SIPC. PAS is a wholly-owned subsidiary of Guardian. North Florida Financial is not an affiliate or subsidiary of PAS or Guardian. This promotional information is not approved or endorsed by the Florida Retirement System or the Division of Retirement. Neither Guardian nor its affiliates are associated with the Florida Retirement System or the Division of Retirement.

John H. Curry
John_Curry@NorthFloridaFinancial.com

The Secure Retirement Method for Members of The Florida Retirement System/ John H. Curry. —1st ed.
ISBN 978-0-9908714-2-2

Contents

How will your retirement measure up?

"People come to me and my team for help in identifying the financial threats to their income and assets. We then co-create a plan to help them eliminate or reduce those financial threats."

John Curry's Secure Retirement Method

The Vision Session

You begin exploring your current situation and new possibilities for your future.

The Discovery Session

A detailed assessment and analysis of your current financial situation and a baseline to build on.

The Strategy Session

A step- by-step planning process to develop strategies, choose tools, and build a team to achieve your goals.

The Implementation Session

A system of tools, resources, capabilities, and expertise for effectively implementing you plans.

John Curry's Secure Retirement Method

Your Retirement Vision

1. Think ahead to the day of your retirement. Looking back from that day what has to have happened along the way for you to feel happy about retirement?

2. What obstacles and concerns stand in your way to achieving your vision of retirement?

3. What are the most important actions you must take to overcome these obstacles and concerns?

4. What progress have you already made toward achieving your retirement vision?

Exclusively for FRS Members

The Secure Retirement Scorecard

Name: _____ Date: _____ Phone: _____

Decide your rating on a scale of 1 (completely disagree with statement) to 10 (completely agree with statement).

	Statement	Rating										Comments
1	I understand the four options under the FRS Pension Plan.	1	2	3	4	5	6	7	8	9	10	
2	I understand my Social Security choices.	1	2	3	4	5	6	7	8	9	10	
3	I understand the Deferred Compensation Program.	1	2	3	4	5	6	7	8	9	10	
4	I understand the DROP Program.	1	2	3	4	5	6	7	8	9	10	
5	I have a step-by-step action plan to achieve my retirement goals.	1	2	3	4	5	6	7	8	9	10	
6	My finances are organized and efficient.	1	2	3	4	5	6	7	8	9	10	
7	I am confident about the performance of my investments.	1	2	3	4	5	6	7	8	9	10	
8	I have a trusted team of advisors helping me achieve my goals.	1	2	3	4	5	6	7	8	9	10	
9	I have a plan to protect and enhance my lifestyle.	1	2	3	4	5	6	7	8	9	10	
10	I have a strong sense of confidence about my future.	1	2	3	4	5	6	7	8	9	10	
Add Column Totals												**Your Score:**

If you would like to discuss your Scorecard, call 850-562-3000 to schedule a phone appointment or email John_Curry@GLIC.com.

INTRODUCTION

This book is intended primarily for members of the Florida Retirement System (FRS), although many of the lessons imparted in this book, on topics like Medicare, Social Security, retirement accounts, taxes, and more, will help anyone concerned about retirement.

Everything in this book, with the exception of the FRS pension, applies to any person who has a job and has some sort of retirement money, whether 401(k), 403(b), IRA, or SEP plan if they're self-employed.

However, as an FRS member, you have many important decisions about how you receive your pension and retirement funds. And you have to take into account how FRS fits in with your overall financial and retirement planning.

Not only have I been working with FRS members for more than 45 years, I have a personal connection to the program, which has inspired me to help people to make the right decisions for their specific needs.

I grew up in a state employee family. My father and grandfather worked their entire careers for the Florida Department of Transportation in DeFuniak Springs, FL.

When my grandfather retired, he chose Option 1 with the State of Florida pension program. He thought he would live a long time after retirement but died shortly before turning 72.

My grandmother lost that pension and lived until just before her 95th birthday. She was without that pension for 27 years and survived on a small Social Security check.

When my dad was looking at retirement he was determined to not make the same mistake as his father. He chose Option 3, and he received a check every month from his retirement at 62 to his death at 85. And that pension continued to my mother until she died four years later.

Which man made the right decision? The truth is that both men made suboptimal decisions. They simply didn't get good advice.

My mission is to help FRS members understand all the options so that you may make an informed, educated decision that fits your specific situation.

Guiding Principles

We all have some vision of retirement. It's my calling to help members of the FRS achieve their vision.

There are unique challenges to retirement planning for FRS members. I'm guided in my work by a set of principles that I adhere to.

1. Protect what you have.
2. Grow the assets.
3. Make sure the assets will pay you income that's reliable, preferably guaranteed.
4. Planning and strategy come before products.

The most important part of retirement planning is to know what your vision of retirement is. You must figure out what retirement means to you. Many people don't actually know what they want out of their retirement beyond some vague notions.

But getting clarity on that point is key and that's the first step I take in helping people, bringing leadership and competence to the table working for you.

For those FRS members, the number one question is: Do you take the pension or investment plan? (Hint: If you're already in the pension, you probably want to stay there.)

Then, for those in the Pension Plan, we talk about the four options and if it makes sense to defer money into the future with a 457 deferred compensation plan, a 403(b) plan, 401(k), or IRA.

Many people have been told to put money into these types of plans because they assume that when you retire, you'll be in a lower tax bracket. But we're not seeing that in practice. Most of the people I work with are in the same tax bracket, if not higher, when they go into retirement. We'll cover more on taxes in Chapter 3.

The Price of Misinformation

Too many people get into situations like this in retirement because they took the advice of well-meaning friends. Keep in mind that something that works for one person might not work the same way for another because of different circumstances, say having other assets, financial products, or income in place.

That's why your retirement plan has to be unique to you and your needs. The purpose of this book is to help you rise above the misinformation and misconceptions about retirement that are out there and give you the facts so you may make informed decisions.

Some other topics we'll discuss will help answer these burning questions:

- At what age should you retire?
- Should you go into the DROP program or keep working?
- At what age should you take Social Security? 62, the earliest you may get it or wait until the full retirement age between 66 and 67... or wait until age 70 so you receive the maximum benefit?[1]
- What about Medicare? Should you choose original Medicare or a Medicare Advantage Plan?
- What do you do with all your retirement money once you're actually retired?
- How do you make sure you don't inadvertently take on a surprise tax burden?
- How do you handle required minimum distributions (RMDs)?

My philosophy is very simple. I'm going to follow the rules, the regulations, and the law. But I'm going to take advantage of anything that allows you to reduce income taxes and have more money for yourself and your family.

We talk a lot about dangers, opportunities, and strengths. My view is to eliminate or reduce dangers, take advantage of the opportunities that are there and

---

[1] https://www.ssa.gov/benefits/retirement/planner/agereduction.html

use your strengths to create benefits for the rest of your life.

Without a plan like this, you'll be confused about the big questions. You could face increased tax liability... you could lose out on a significant portion of monthly income... you could pay more for healthcare and prescriptions than you have to...

Your retirement could not be the one you envisioned.

But with a clearly defined plan, you can avoid all of that.

CHAPTER 1

The Florida Retirement System Pension Program

The Florida Retirement System was created in 1970[2] as an attempt by the state to bring all existing plans for state employees together.

Until 1975, the plan was contributory, which meant you had to put in some of your own money. After that, the State of Florida totally funded the program until 2011, when employees were compelled to contribute 3%.[3]

---

[2] https://www.myfrs.com/FRSPro_Pension.htm#how
[3] https://www.mybenefits.myflorida.com/financial_future/frs_investment_plan

Your Contribution

Some FRS members are angry that they have to contribute 3% to the pension plan. Personally, I think that it's the responsibility of every member. You have to have a little bit of skin in the game, so to speak. And you should understand it's just another way of making sure the plan is more solvent to take care of not only you, but the people behind you.

The FRS Pension Plan is a defined benefit plan, in which you are guaranteed a benefit at retirement if you meet certain criteria. The amount of your future benefit is determined by a formula, based on your earnings, length of service, and membership class.

Your benefit is pre-funded by contributions paid by your employer. The Florida Retirement System must ensure that sufficient funds are available when your benefits are due and bears the market risk and investment decisions.

Who Is Eligible?

All FRS employees are eligible for the Pension Plan except:

- Mandatory State University System Optional Retirement Program (SUSORP) members. (This is not an FRS plan.)
- Teachers' Retirement System members. (This plan is closed.)[4]

How Your Benefit Accumulates

In the Pension Plan, your benefits are generally "backloaded," which means that you accumulate benefits slowly at first and then at a faster rate the longer you stay. This is different from the Investment Plan, where benefits are earned more or less evenly over your career (subject to fluctuations in the financial markets and your investment strategy)

When You Own Your Pension Plan Benefit

You will be eligible for a Pension Plan benefit (i.e. be vested) when you complete six years of service (if you were enrolled in the FRS prior to July 1, 2011) or eight years of service (if you were enrolled in the FRS on or after July 1, 2011). If you terminated FRS-covered employment before July 1, 2001, vesting varied based on membership class:

---

[4] https://www.myfrs.com/FRSPro_Pension.htm#who

- Members of the Regular Class, Special Risk Class and Special Risk Administrative Support Class vested in the FRS Pension Plan after completing 10 years of creditable service.
- Members of the Elected Officers' Class vested in the FRS Pension Plan after completing eight years of creditable service.
- Members of the Senior Management Service Class vested in the FRS Pension Plan after completing seven years of creditable service.[5]

If you use your 2nd Choice option to transfer from the FRS Investment Plan to the FRS Pension Plan, you will be able to count your Investment Plan service toward the vesting requirement.

The 4 Options under the FRS Pension

There have been many changes to the program over the years, including some significant ones made by the Florida Legislature in 2011,[6] that impact people. The result is a lot of confusion.

---

[5] https://www.myfrs.com/FRSPro_ComparePlan_Vesting.htm
[6]https://www.myfrs.com/imageserver/plumtree/remote/custom/201 1_Legislation_Summary.pdf-old

It always surprises me how little FRS members know about the program, which is why many people don't know which option to choose.

There are four options under the Florida Retirement System pension program.

A FRS member must select one of the following retirement options prior to receipt of their first monthly retirement benefit:

Option 1:

A monthly benefit payable for your lifetime. Upon your death the monthly benefit will stop, and your beneficiary will receive only a refund of any contributions you have paid which are in excess of the amount you have received in benefits. This option does not provide a continuing benefit to your beneficiary.

Option 2:

A reduced monthly benefit payable for your lifetime. If you die within a period of 10 years after your retirement date, your designated beneficiary will receive a monthly benefit in the same amount as you were receiving for the balance of the 10-year period. No further benefits are paid to your surviving spouse.

Option 3:

A reduced monthly benefit payable for your lifetime. When you die, your joint annuitant, if living, will receive a lifetime monthly benefit payment in the same amount as you were receiving.

(Exception: The benefit paid to a joint annuitant who is not your spouse and under age 25 will be your Option One benefit amount. The benefit will stop when your joint annuitant reaches age 25, unless they are disabled and incapable of self-support. In that case, the benefit will continue for the duration of the disability.) No further benefits are payable to anyone after both you and your joint annuitant are deceased.

Option 4:

An adjusted monthly benefit payable to you while both you and your joint annuitant are living. Upon the death of either you or your joint annuitant, the monthly benefit payable to the surviving person is reduced to two-thirds of the monthly benefit payable while you were both living.

No further benefits are payable after both you and your joint annuitant are deceased. The same exception as in Option 3 applies.[7]

---

[7] https://www.myfrs.com/FRSPro_ComparePlan_Payment.htm

A Case Study in the 4 Options

As I mentioned in the introduction, I have some personal experience with FRS pensions and the potential consequences of choosing certain options.

Option 1

When my grandfather retired from the Department of Transportation, he chose Option 1. This is the maximum benefit, and you receive that check as long as you live. The day you die, it dies with you.

Unfortunately, he died soon after he retired, leaving my grandmother with no pension for more than 27 years. So it's an expensive option if you don't live a long time.

But if you live to 100, you get that check every month.

Why did he choose this option? I think it's worth exploring because I see many people in my practice have the same mindset. He wanted the most money, and he didn't really think much about what would happen after he died. It would be one thing if he had a large life insurance policy, but he did not.

Option 2

This is also a lifetime benefit, with an important difference from Option 1. It's a lifetime benefit to the employee, with 10 years certain to their beneficiary. So, in the case of my grandfather who died five years into retirement, my grandmother would have received the pension for another five years.

Option 3

This option is joint, with 100% to the survivor. This is what my dad chose. It does give less income, about 15% less than the maximum benefit offered in Option 1. My father saw the consequence of my grandfather's decision. Taking care of his family after he was gone was important. This may be a good option for someone without a life insurance policy or significant savings or investments.

Option 4

This option causes a lot of confusion. Basically, the member gets the full check until they die. At that point, the joint annuitant gets 2/3 of that amount for the rest of their life. However, many don't realize that if your joint annuitant dies first, generally the spouse, the FRS member's check is also reduced to 2/3.

I've had people come to my office angry that the State of Florida misled them or their spouse about the options. But I have to tell them that it's all right there in bold print.

What happened, in many cases, was that they saw that the benefit in Option 1 was much bigger in dollars. And they locked into that without considering what happened to their spouse after. Or they chose Option 4, thinking that upon their death, their surviving spouse could live on less. But they didn't consider what would happen if their spouse died first and their benefit was reduced.

It's pretty sobering when you have to have these conversations. But this is a perfect example of why members of the FRS need to be informed.

The first time they read about the plan and the different options shouldn't be the day before retirement because they're almost guaranteed to be making an uninformed decision. It could work out fine... or it could have a tremendous impact on your retirement and/or your spouse's life.

Cost of Living Benefit

Depending on when you entered the Florida Retirement System, you might have an annual cost of living adjustment benefit for any of the four options you choose. It was a flat 3% annual increase. But on July 1, 2011 that changed. If you were hired after that date, there is no cost of living adjustment in retirement. Many people don't know this.[8]

Even if you are eligible for the cost of living adjustment, it is being scaled down.

Which Option Should You Choose?

It's important to note that none of these options are better than another. They're all good in certain circumstances because they're designed for different purposes.

The challenge is choosing one of the four options that works for you and then, because they don't operate in a vacuum, coordinating with your Social Security benefit, your life insurance, your deferred compensation, your IRA, or 401(k), your savings and your investments.

---

[8] https://www.myfrs.com/FRSPro_ComparePlan_Cost.htm

All of these elements have to be reviewed together as a total package in order to create a comprehensive retirement plan that will last you the rest of your life.

And consider this: most people live probably 20 to 25 years or even longer in retirement. On average, we are living longer. So if you're going to be living in retirement for 30 years, your plan better work from day one.

Should There Be a Pension Plan?

Corporate America gave up most pension benefits back in the 1980s in favor of the defined contribution plan called the 401(k).

I'm convinced that there will be more and more pressure put on states, including Florida, to get rid of the pension plan and have more of what we have now with the Florida Retirement System Investment Plan. As with private-sector retirement accounts, this is a defined contribution plan to which the employer and employee contribute. The money is invested.

A new hire in the state of Florida today may choose either to join the pension plan or the investment plan. If you know you're not staying until you are vested in the pension plan, which is after eight years, you might want to take the investment plan.

The State Board of Administration does all the investing in the Pension Plan, and they're responsible for backing up the income. In 2008, pensions took a big hit. Today, there's worry about whether pensions are solvent. Meaning, can they meet the obligations into the future?

I can't speak for the State of Florida. I can't speak for the State Board of Administration. But I think they're doing a good job. And I think people who dig deep into the health of the plan will see that our pension plan for our state employees in Florida is better than most.

Your Decision

The plan document for the FRS pension options is very complicated. And the decision becomes even more complicated when you try to coordinate with your Social Security, other retirement accounts, assets, and other income sources.

To be successful, you need to do more than just look at four numbers on a piece of paper representing the money you get each month from each option. The option you choose should be part of a comprehensive retirement income plan, which is what we are exploring in this book.

CHAPTER 2

Should You Go Into DROP?

The DROP, or Deferred Retirement Option Program, allows employees who are eligible to retire to continue to work and <u>earn retirement benefits.</u>

Your monthly retirement benefits aren't paid to you directly but instead go in the FRS Trust Fund, where they will earn interest (currently 1.3%), tax deferred, for as long as you are in the program and continue to work for an FRS employer, which is a specified and limited period. You may be in the program for up to 60 months (five years).

Basically you are earning credit towards your future retirement benefit, which is calculated at the time you start in DROP, plus cost of living adjustments. Once you're done, whatever is in your DROP accounts is paid as either:

- A lump sum, with 20% withheld for taxes
- A rollover to any retirement plan that will accept it, like an IRA, 457 deferred compensation plan, FRS investment plan, or 401(k).
- A combination partial lump sum and rollover

In most cases, you have to choose to enter DROP within 12 months of hitting your normal retirement age.[9]

There are many considerations as to whether you should take advantage of this program. And you have to think beyond the money.

When people come into my office talking about DROP, they're on one of two ends of the spectrum.

Many hesitate because they're not sure they want to leave in five years. Because once you go into the DROP you have to leave at five years, if not sooner. I've had a lot of people tell me they regret going into DROP because they loved their job.

But it's tempting because you have this opportunity to receive a big bucket of money... maybe the largest bucket of money you've ever had at one time in your life.

---

[9]https://www.dms.myflorida.com/workforce_operations/retirement/active_members/deferred_retirement_option_program_drop

On the other side you have people who say that they absolutely hate their jobs, they can't stand it anymore, and they want to get out as quickly as possible. Yet, these folks are also tempted by this bucket of money.

They have a decision to make. Do they continue working longer and not do DROP and retire in a year or two? Do they go into DROP knowing that they may not finish the full five years because they really don't like their job?

DROP... Or Not?

Do you like your job? If you like it enough to stay another 10, 15, or 20 years, you probably shouldn't do DROP.

If you went into DROP you would have a lump sum. You have to ask yourself if it's worth having that money to walk away after five years. Some people say no, I love my job. If that's the case, DROP isn't for you.

Some say, I don't want to stay in this job. I want to retire from the State of Florida and do other things, like maybe start a business. In that case, you should consider DROP seriously so you can get the lump sum that accumulates tax deferred.

What many people don't understand is that when they enter into DROP, they've had to choose one of the four options for the FRS pension plan because they are, for all intents and purposes, retired and now participating in the Deferred Retirement Option Plan.

You don't want to make the wrong choice, because you might hurt yourself or your spouse, like we talked about my grandfather taking Option 1 and my grandmother losing that income for the rest of her life because he didn't live as long as he expected.

Whether or not to join DROP is a personal decision that you must make based on your retirement goals – and how much you like your job.

Already in DROP? Here's What You Need to Know

If you're already in the middle of DROP, looking to the future… what should you do when you get the money? Do you take a lump sum and pay all the taxes today? I have had clients who have done so in order to pay off debt or make a large purchase.

In my opinion, most people should defer that tax even further by placing the money in another tax deferred retirement plan like an IRA where it may continue to grow, and then take income from that as required minimum distributions at age 72.

I think most people approach DROP the wrong way: an opportunity to quit working and have a big bucket of money. The reason DROP came into being was to encourage people to retire to get rid of us "old folks" and bring in new people to state government.

It should have been a temporary program to get people out and bring new people in. But it's there. And as long as it's there, you should participate in it, if it fits.

CHAPTER 3

Tax Considerations in Retirement, Including 457 Plans, 403(b)s, 401(k)s, IRAs, and More

There's a lot of talk about taxes these days, as always. Will they be raised… lowered… nobody really can predict what will take flight on the political winds out there. But that's not what we're concerned with here. We're focused on the actions we can take, and what we can control.

We are most interested in how taxes may impact your retirement… and they can have a huge impact – a negative one, if you don't make the appropriate preparations.

The biggest question: Should you pay your taxes to-day... or should you defer them into the future?

"When you retire, will you be in the same tax bracket as today? If not, will it be higher or lower?"

The answer, as with everything I share in this book, is it depends.

Before we dig deeper into taxes, a question for you: When you retire, will you be in the same tax bracket as today? If not, will it be higher or lower?

When you retire, every day is "Saturday." What do you do on Saturdays? You go places, eat out, do fun things... and spend money. Most people don't realize that they'll want more income, not less, in retirement.

I have people tell me they want to be in a lower tax bracket when they retire, and I tell them they don't need me. Because if you're in a lower tax bracket, that means you have less income. And that's not what I help people with. My job is to help you retire with as much income as possible. Preferably, at least what you were earning before you retired, not less.

Retirement gives you a lot of free time. Don't you want the income to truly enjoy it?

I'll admit, this attitude puzzles people, probably because they've been taught that when you retire, the conventional thinking is that you'll get about 50% of your working income with your pension, if you have one, plus a bit more with Social Security. So you must prepare to settle for about 70% of your job income.

But why would you start there? Why don't we start with 100% or better? Admittedly, that won't happen for everyone. But why not make that your goal and not settle for 70%.

Another consideration...

What will your income be when you retire?

What will the tax brackets be?

To answer those questions, it helps to have some context.

A Little Bit of History

When I used to teach continuing education for CPAs, I would ask the class, "Who can tell me what was the top marginal tax bracket since Congress passed the 16th amendment in 1913?" Nobody ever got it right.

The top bracket, in 1944, during World War II, was 94%. Let's talk a little history to get context.

When I was getting my master's degree in financial services, we had one entire course, not a class – an entire course, just on the history of our income tax. It is fascinating.

Income tax in our country came with the passage of the 16th amendment. The top tax bracket in that year was 7%. To get there you had to earn $500,000 or more a year.

In the press, the headlines said it was a temporary tax. And it was. It held at 7% for three years. In year four, they raised it to 15%. Why? Well, they needed more money to finance some things like World War I. Tax rates went up.

Then during the Great Depression income tax rates were 25%. All of this data is available on the IRS website.[10]

I find it interesting when people talk about taxing the high-income people, the wealthy people. Because if you look at the same charts I see, the tax rates went up higher for those folks. But guess what? The tax rates came up

---

[10] https://www.irs.gov/statistics/soi-tax-stats-historical-table-23

for everybody. Maybe not as severe, but they still came up.

And even though in the 1980s Ronald Reagan pounded Congress to drop the top bracket from 50%, down to 28%, which was helpful, that did not mean we paid less in tax. In fact, most of us did not pay less tax.[11] Why? Because they were controlling the levers; they dropped the tax bracket.

But they took away deductions.

I'm not a tax attorney; I'm not a CPA. I do have a Master of Science in Financial Services. And I enjoy reading about and studying these topics and teaching it as much as I can. I am convinced that if we really understood what's happening to us, there would be another revolution. Know this: taxes are inevitable. You can't control them. But you can control your response.

Making Tax Decisions Today to Control Your Future

All this sets the stage for the question: Should you pay taxes today or defer them to the future using 401(k)s, 457 deferred compensation plans, 403(b)s, IRAs, or other retirement tools?

---

[11] https://www.investopedia.com/terms/t/taxreformact1986.asp

It comes down to many factors:

What will your tax bracket be?

What does the tax law allow you to deduct or not deduct?

Anytime you change administrations, or Congress, there is a lot of bickering over tax rates.

That means we don't know what your taxes will be in the future. However, I hope that with the planning we do together, you're in the maximum tax bracket. But we'll look for opportunities to minimize the tax and avoid the tax. Not evade – avoid. Because the difference between evading and avoiding could be time in prison.

For folks in the Florida Retirement System, you have options. There are plans where you may defer your compensation and you may defer your tax payments.

457 Deferred Compensation Plans[12]

The most basic option is the 457 deferred compensation plan, which most FRS members are familiar with. It's simple. You set aside money for retirement that

---

[12] https://www.irs.gov/retirement-plans/irc-457b-deferred-compensation-plans

comes out of your paycheck automatically as a payroll reduction.

So you take that $100 or $500 or whatever the amount is per month, and it's invested. The State of Florida has different companies they've chosen to be sponsors of their deferred compensation plan.

Then when you retire, every dollar you take out is subject to income tax. In reality, 457 plans are designed to supplement your retirement income.

The Roth 457[13]

With a Roth 457 plan you contribute to your 457 account on an after-tax basis. But when the money is withdrawn you pay no income taxes. This could be an option for reducing taxes in retirement.

403(b) Plans[14]

Employees in the school system, university system, and community college system, as well as state government, have the 403(b) plan, a tax deferred arrangement,

---

[13] https://www.irs.gov/retirement-plans/roth-acct-in-your-retirement-plan

[14] https://www.irs.gov/retirement-plans/irc-403b-tax-sheltered-annuity-plans

also known as tax-sheltered annuity. They are invested in annuities or mutual funds, and the employees are allowed to contribute part of their salary.

(People in the private sector, civilians as I like to call us, may have a 401(k) or IRA. If you're self-employed, you may have a Simplified Employee Pension (SEP) plan.)

401(k)[15]

This is an employer-sponsored defined contribution pension plan. Funds are withdrawn from the employee's paycheck and are often matched at some percentage by the employer. The taxes on the money are deferred until it is withdrawn.

Why the odd name? Like these other plans, it's a reference to its section in the Internal Revenue Code.

IRA[16]

With an Individual Retirement Arrangement contributions are tax deductible, and interest, dividends, and gains are not taxed while the money is in the account. However, when you withdraw the funds you do pay income tax.

---

[15] https://www.irs.gov/retirement-plans/401k-plans
[16] https://www.irs.gov/retirement-plans/individual-retirement-arrangements-iras

Roth IRA[17]

This type of IRA differs from a 401(k) and traditional IRA in that the money in the account is not taxed when distributed as long as the account holder is more than 59 ½ years old or the withdrawal is only from the principal. However, total contributions are restricted – for 2020, it was $7,000 per year for people aged 50 and above. And contributions are not tax deductible.

The Roth IRA was introduced in 1997 with the Taxpayer Relief Act and first available in 1998.[18]

SEP Plan[19]

This Simplified Employee Pension is for business owners and self-employed people – and their employees – to provide retirement benefits. Contributions are tax deductible, and there are higher yearly contribution limits than IRAs. Once the funds are deposited, however, it becomes like a traditional IRA and the same rules are enforced.

---

[17] https://www.irs.gov/retirement-plans/roth-iras

[18] https://www.investopedia.com/terms/t/taxpayer-relief-act-of-1997.asp

[19] https://www.irs.gov/retirement-plans/retirement-plans-faqs-regarding-seps

How These Plans Work

With all of these, you have the same general guidelines. If you put the money in today, you would pay no tax on that contribution until you take it out (except for the Roth IRA). People think that's a great deal. And it is, *if* you are in a lower tax bracket when you retire. If you retire and you are in the same tax bracket or higher... then maybe it's not the best strategy.

In that case, maybe you'd be better off taking the money, paying tax on it, and doing something else with it, like a Roth IRA. I'm genuinely surprised at the number of people who don't use Roth IRAs. Their mindset is that they'd rather "save" on the taxes. But I have news for you, you're not saving taxes, you're *deferring* the tax.

I'm guilty of it myself. I put money in my 401(k)s. But I made sure I have a Roth IRA, and I also have life insurance that builds cash value I may use in the future. So I paid the tax and bought the insurance, because it allows me to do other things in retirement that I can't do if I don't have life insurance.

Defined Benefit Plans vs.

Defined Contribution Plans

All retirement plans come under two categories. It's either a defined benefit plan, like the FRS pension, or a defined contribution plan, like a 401(k) or the FRS Investment Plan.

The defined benefit is based on a formula based on number of years of service, your income and a factor. Basically, you get a percentage of your income paid out to you.

A defined contribution plan, like the FRS Investment Plan or a 401(k) is different. What you get out of these plans is based on how much money you put in and the performance of the investments. You as the employee have the pressure and the burden of handling that money to make sure it lasts you for your lifetime.

On the other hand, the pension takes away all of the investment decisions. Because the State Board of Administration does all the investing, and they're responsible for backing up the income.

Other Tax Issues

I believe in talking about the good, the bad and the ugly with everything we're doing regarding your retirement. What does that mean? Too many times people will tell us what's good about something, they never tell us what's bad. And I always like to ask the question, "Well, tell me what's ugly about it." Don't just give me the good stuff. Tell me everything.

If you work with me, you'll hear it all. The good, the bad and the ugly. I call that the Clint Eastwood method.

I think it's just important to understand that if we look back at our tax history. When the tax rates went up, it was because Congress was spending a lot of money or various presidential administrations were. Money had to be collected in the form of taxes to pay for that spending.

If you look at what's happening in our environment today, I don't see how any reasonable person could say that our tax rates won't go up. I believe during my life-time, I will see tax rates back to 50%, if not higher, maybe 70%. Because there's a lot of pressure to collect more. At some point, tax rates have to go up, because the members of Congress are not willing to make some of the tough decisions that have to be made because they're worried about not getting reelected.

Do You Have a Choice?

Some people have the choice to have both 457 plans and 403(b)s, as well as other retirement accounts.

Whether you do or not really comes down to what your employer offers.

When I meet with people, I ask these questions:

- What are you trying to accomplish?
- Are you looking for growth at all costs?
- Are you looking for moderate growth?
- Are you looking for guarantees?

One last thought...

I had considered including information here on the contribution limits and various rules for these plans. However, by the time you read this, the law may have changed. The rules are constantly changing. If you're saying, "Hey, I'm in state government, and they won't change for me," consider that there was a major change to your FRS Pension Plan in July 2011.

My recommendation is to review each of your plans on a regular basis to keep track of limits and any new rules that are implemented that apply to you.

CHAPTER 4

At What Age Should You Retire?

As you consider your retirement planning, one of the most important decisions you'll make is *when* you retire. When you can start collecting Social Security, withdrawing funds from retirement accounts, and get on Medicare will impact that decision.

But I also believe you can't answer that question until you determine what retirement looks like for you. I call that your "retirement mindset," and everybody has different thoughts on this.

I have a passion for what I do. I decided many years ago that my primary focus would be on retirement income planning.

What everybody that I work with has in common is that someday they want to retire. That's true for my FRS clients, those in the university system and schoolteachers, as well as the business owners, doctors, lawyers, and others I work with.

The question is, what does that look like? And that's the first place I'll start with people, which makes me quite different than most of the folks who claim to be doing retirement planning.

I believe it's not just about the money. The money finances your retirement. And you want enough to maintain the quality of life you desire.

I always ask why you want to retire in the first place, and then that helps us determine when you should retire.

When you think of a financial advisor, you probably think of somebody who is going to help you with specific things like choosing life insurance or managing investments – specific tasks like that.

The Whole Financial Picture of Your Life

I take a more holistic approach. I want to know what you're trying to accomplish, your vision of retirement, and why you're seeking help. Before we get into how to invest your money and how you spend your money, let's talk about what you're trying to get done.

And before we make any decisions on certain products to use or strategies to implement, we look at everything – your whole financial picture.

- Protections like car insurance, homeowner's insurance, health insurance, disability income insurance, and life insurance...
- Assets like savings, investments, retirement plans, real estate, and business interests...
- Obligations and liabilities like taxes, credit cards, mortgages, car loans, and more...
- Then we look at what your cash flow is today and how much you are saving for the future...

We're facing unbelievable pressure in this day and age.

I tell everybody that you can't control any of that. All you can control is your personal economy. If you stick your head in the sand like an ostrich with your butt sticking out, I've got news for you, you're vulnerable.

Take the time to plan for yourself. And if you work with me, the first thing I'm going to ask you is to tell me what the future looks like. Tell me what you want. What does retirement mean to you? What's your vision of retirement?

Many people haven't really thought about what they're going to do in retirement. They have the party, get the "gold watch"... and then wake up the next day and say, "Now what?"

I want to know what you plan to do after you retire from the State of Florida and start taking your pension. Will you fully retire?

Or do you see yourself doing something else? Maybe working part-time to pursue one of your passions. Or maybe you want to start a business or consulting practice. It's very possible you may take what you learned from your experiences at your job and take that into the world and get paid for it.

Perhaps you want to be productive but not in a job or business. You don't have to work for a paycheck; you might volunteer. I know people who do a lot of volunteer work at churches and other nonprofit organizations.

The bottom-line is that you shouldn't spend or invest $1 until you're totally clear on what you want your retirement to be. Once you are clear, everything comes into focus.

Let me use myself as an example.

At the time of this writing, I'm 68. On paper, I'm retired. I'm taking Social Security and a pension. I'm on Medicare. But I never fully retired. I think about four freedoms in relation to retirement.

1. Relationships

I love my work, but I'm to the point in my life where I don't have to take on a new client. If it's not a good fit, I won't take them and will even refer them to an associate. Why complicate my life? I want to focus on relationships with the best-fit clients – and my family and friends.

2. Time

I want the time to do things I want to do. Again, I don't take on work that I won't enjoy.

3. Money

Having guaranteed income streams allows me to enjoy the time that I have. My own retirement planning has given me this ability.

4. Location

I can do what I do... wherever I want. I'm not tied to one location.

In short, in my retirement, I will continue to work on my passion of retirement income planning, I want to work when and where I want to work with whom I want to work. Of course, some people just want to be done with work forever and fully retire.

Retiring for the Wrong Reasons

Sometimes people come to my office angry and frustrated. They want to retire because they hate their job.

It sounds like they're talking about a prison sentence, the way they describe it. I tell them if that's how they feel maybe they should just retire tomorrow. They tell me they can't afford to. I tell them that maybe that's not true... that we could look at all their financials and maybe they actually could retire now.

That doesn't mean they should. The ability to retire when you want could give you quite a bit of leverage to improve the situation at work.

One of my clients recently reminded me of a conversation we had nine years ago. I told him he could afford to retire. So he told his boss that the next day and said that if he wanted him to stay, these are the changes that had to happen in the workplace. If not, he said he would head right over to human resources and file his paperwork to retire.

That compelled his boss to sit down and listen to his concerns and they worked out their disagreements. He ended up working another two years, and he was glad to because once the issues were sorted out, he genuinely enjoyed the work.

So he got more benefits for himself and the organization he worked for benefited. His boss even got another promotion because of him staying.

I was able to do the same thing with a woman who was also "unable" to retire. I was able to reach her by hitting her hot button: travel. She wanted to travel more. She wanted to go back to Europe. I said, "What's stopping you?" She said she had to go to work. I asked, "Do you *have* to work… or do you *choose* to work?"

Why didn't these people just retire?

It gets back to the concept of mindset that I've been talking about.

Some people have the ability to retire financially. But they don't have the ability to mentally retire.

That's part of my role as a financial advisor. I sit down with you like a coach and challenge your thinking in an unemotional, non-judgmental way and look at your situation holistically.

So if you're thinking that you have no future in your current job, I can help talk you through it and help you create your future. Because it's sad not to have a future.

I can't make you do anything. All I can do is guide you, coach you based on my expertise, education, and life experiences, as well as the knowledge and wisdom that I've gained by helping so many people in my more than 45 years in business.

Here's what I've learned in all that time: I do not take responsibility for anyone who won't take action and help themselves.

I'm here when you want me. I'll help you any way I can. But I can't do it for you. I'll do it with you.

CHAPTER 5

When Should You Start Taking Social Security?

Social Security is a complicated topic, and it's becoming a more and more important issue, especially with all the changes in recent years.

Politicians are kicking around ideas about changing Social Security, the income base for taxes is going up... and that's just the start of the many ongoing issues with this program.

It's always on people's minds and for good reason.

For many, Social Security is the only guaranteed lifelong income they have. Folks with a pension like the Florida Retirement System have two. But if you're self-employed or if you're in a job without a pension, it may be your only lifetime reliable income stream.

Along with a 401(k) 457 deferred comp plan, IRA, Roth IRA, or 403(b)... whatever you have... the burden on you is to make it last for the rest of your life. The first question most people have about Social Security is when they should start taking it.

The earliest you may go on Social Security is age 62. You may also wait until full retirement age, which is between 66 and 67. It depends on the year you were born. The maximum benefit is paid at 70.

There is no reduction in benefits or penalty as long as you are at full retirement age or older when you start taking Social Security.

Ages for Eligibility for Full Social Security Benefits[20]

Birth Year	Full Retirement Age
1943 – 1954	66
1955	66 and 2 months
1956	66 and 4 months
1957	66 and 6 months
1958	66 and 8 months
1959	66 and 10 months
1960 and later	67

However, between age 62, when you are first eligible, and your full retirement age, there is a reduction. At that

---

[20] https://www.ssa.gov/pubs/EN-05-10035.pdf

age, you are collecting roughly 75% of what you benefit could have been if you waited until your full retirement age.

That's a 25% reduction for the rest of your life. You can see why that one decision can have a huge impact on your retirement.

In this chapter, we'll talk about how Social Security is taxed, and what happens whether you are married, divorced, or your spouse dies before you or vice-versa (the widow or widower's benefit).

There is a lot of misinformation on all these topics, especially with recent changes.

I'll also touch on the cost of living adjustment. Again, a lot of misinformation out there. Many people assume that the cost of living adjustment goes up every year by law. The reality is that it's not a law, there's a provision for this increase. But you don't always get an adjustment every year. It's at the discretion of the Social Security Administration.

Let's go back to 2009. The cost of living adjustment that year was 5.8%. And that's hard to believe, because remember what the economy looked like in 2008, 2009.

I think that was Congress's way of saying we've got to do something because people are in trouble financially. But then in 2010, and 2011, zero cost of living adjustment, nothing. And then it was 3.6. And then it hovered around 1.7%. Then in 2016, zero again, for 2020, they raised it 1.6%[21]

Even if you get a cost of living adjustment, that doesn't mean your net income will increase. My premiums went up for Medicare Part B.

The Right Time to Take Social Security for You

Now, let's tackle one of the most important decisions you'll make in retirement: when you should start taking your Social Security benefit.

As you might expect, there's no one right answer for everybody. And first, you need to determine if you'll still be working when you take Social Security, full-time or part-time, and what income level.

Are you aware there is a penalty if you're making above a certain amount and receive Social Security? If you're younger than full retirement age for all of the previous year, you'll lose $1 for every $2 you earn above the limit, which is $18,240 (in 2020), at age 62 until you

---

[21] https://www.ssa.gov/oact/cola/latestCOLA.html

reach your full retirement age. If you've heard people say they can't make more than $18,000 per year in retirement, they're referring to this earnings limit. Social Security will deduct $1 from your benefits for every $3 you earn that year above $48,600 (in 2020) until you reach full retirement age.[22]

There is no cap on your income after you reach full retirement age. You may earn as much as you want and receive your full Social Security benefit.

An important factor in your decision to take Social Security is what your total financial picture looks like.

- What assets do you have?
- What income do you need?
- What happens in the event of your death?
- What will your spouse get?

For people without adequate life insurance, I tell them they should delay Social Security as long as possible because the Social Security benefit will be very important to their surviving spouse.

If someone doesn't have a good life insurance program and they've got very little savings, I encourage

---

[22]https://www.ssa.gov/benefits/retirement/planner/whileworking.html

them to work to 70. For someone who doesn't have these issues, I recommend they collect at full retirement age.

Every year you wait from full retirement age to age 70, you get an 8% increase in your Social Security benefit. In my case, I took mine at 66. I could have waited until 70 and gotten 32% more; 8 x 4 = 32. After working for 45 years, I said, "I want mine now." With that money, sometimes I'll pay for life insurance, put it in savings, add it to my investments, or take care of my grandchildren.[23]

Another issue is we're living longer on average. In my case, if I live to life expectancy, I'm pretty much going to break even – receive the same total amount – as if I had waited until age 70. Social Security uses 83 for their life expectancy for men and women.[24]

That's something you must consider. There are no guarantees, of course, as to how long you'll live. But if you're healthy, and you appear to have longevity on your side, do you want to start taking your benefit at full retirement age and get it longer? Or do you wait until age 70 and get the higher amount for a shorter period of time?

---

[23] https://www.ssa.gov/pubs/EN-05-10035.pdf
[24] https://www.ssa.gov/oact/population/longevity.html

Based on your other income and assets, you may not need Social Security until 70. In my case, I had the assets and I'm still working, but I want the money now. But I didn't take it until 66 because I would have gotten a reduction because of my earnings.

Tax Considerations

First, let's get this out of the way, because somehow some people don't realize it. When you start collecting Social Security, it will be taxed.

Depending upon your income level, an individual may be taxed on up to 50% of their benefit. A married couple, as high as 85% of income from Social Security could be taxed. There's a formula that your CPA or the person who does your taxes can calculate for you. But the bottom line is a married couple earning over a certain amount of income – I won't get into specifics because it changes – but you may find that up to 85% of your Social Security benefit is considered income for tax purposes.

So you take 85% of your benefit, multiply it by whatever your tax bracket is, and you just watch that money go right back to the government.[25]

---

[25] https://www.ssa.gov/benefits/retirement/planner/taxes.html

What Happens When You Die?

If you've been married for 10 years, or more, then upon your death, your spouse would be entitled to a widow or widower benefit – a spousal benefit. While living in retirement, your spouse will be entitled to a retirement benefit based on either their earnings if it is higher or yours if yours is higher.[26]

I'll admit, this rule is a little confusing. For example, I just had a situation where a man died. The wife thought she was going to collect his full Social Security benefit. However, she did not because of her age and the amount of money she earned.

Congress makes changes in the details of Social Security from time to time. Sometimes it's widely reported, sometimes not. And that means what people think they know about Social Security might not be correct.

Myself, I have to stay updated all the time. The Social Security Administration has more than 5,000 rules and regulations. To make matters worse, even when you call Social Security, you talk to one person, you get one answer, talk to another, you get a different answer.

---

[26] https://www.ssa.gov/oact/progdata/benefits.html

So it's truly up to the individual retiree to do their homework and get some expert help. Full disclosure, I don't claim to be an expert on Social Security. But I am pretty darn good at it.

Admittedly, I don't have access to any more "insider" information than the average person. I still go on the website. But I will tell you that I'm part of a study group that pays close attention to what's happening with Social Security, Medicare, tax planning, and retirement planning in general.

If you think about it, Congress doesn't like to publicize when they make changes with Social Security because it's going to ruffle feathers. What's interesting is that in the '80s, there was hardly any press coverage about the changes in Social Security... even though there were major changes.

Will Social Security Ever Go Away?

I hear from people in Generation X and younger, who think that by the time they come to retirement age, Social Security will not exist because the current group of retirees will get it all.

I do not think we'll ever see Social Security go away. But I believe there will be some major changes. In my opinion, they should have happened long ago, but neither political party wanted to tackle it. We should have never been allowed to collect Social Security at 62. It was never designed for that. Congress let that happen, and that's when we started seeing problems with Social Security.

Now, if you took away Social Security at age 62, that would kick up one heck of a fuss because many people count on that benefit. So, I'm not sure what the answer is.

But I do know this. Back in 1983, there were major changes to Social Security, including an increase in the payroll tax rate, full retirement age was increased, and up to 50% of the value of your benefit was made taxable income.[27] In 2015, in Congress there were bipartisan changes to Social Security meant to close so-called loopholes that allowed people to secure benefits that were not intended to be part of the program, including the practices of aggressive claiming. They got it to a vote in two weeks, and they were implemented.[28]

The point is that things are moving faster, these changes are being made quickly, because more lawmakers are realizing that if we don't fix it, Social Security will be in trouble.

---

[27] https://www.ssa.gov/history/1983amend.html
[28] https://www.ssa.gov/legislation/legis_bulletin_110315.html

If you go to the official Social Security website and read the Trustee's Report, you'll get matter-of-fact information and an assessment. They're very forthright in saying that by 2033 or 2034, the system will only be able to pay about 70% of current benefits.[29]

That means in this scenario that Social Security recipients at that time will have to accept a reduction in their benefits.

Only time will tell if that happens. However, that possibility is something you should consider when to start taking this benefit. Some people advocate that you should take it as soon as possible because they maintain the program will go bankrupt, so you better get in to get all you can. I don't agree.

How Much You Will Get From Social Security?

Go to the Retirement Calculator at www.ssa.gov/myaccount to get an estimate of your personal retirement benefits, and to see the effects of different retirement age scenarios.

---

[29] https://www.ssa.gov/oact/trsum/

CHAPTER 6

There's More to Medicare Than Meets the Eye

Healthcare costs are one of the biggest concerns for people going into retirement. For many folks, it is their biggest expense in retirement. You want to know if you'll be able to cover the price of the medical care you'll need as you age, especially in the face of ever-rising healthcare costs.

We may debate what type of healthcare is needed in this country all day long. But as with everything I've talked about in this book, you have to take care of your own personal economy and make a plan that takes care of you first. You don't know what's going to happen with the government; you can't control it.

Medicare is of vital importance to most seniors. Think of it as being our country's federal health insurance program for people that are 65 or older. In some exceptions, younger people may benefit too.

As with many things about retirement, there is a lot of misunderstanding about this program. You might think, as many do, that there are only two parts to Medicare, A and B. But there are actually four, with C and D. Then you may also purchase a Medicare Supplement policy to fill the gaps in your coverage, often called Medigap insurance, for which you pay premiums.[30]

Why would you pay extra? So you have the ability to get service and full benefits without paying out of pocket, except for the beginning of the year when you do have to pay your deductible. It's a way to control your healthcare costs.

Parts A and B are what is commonly referred to as original Medicare.[31]

Part A

Part A happens pretty much automatically at age 65 if you're in the Social Security system. This covers what's called hospital insurance. It helps pay for inpatient care in a hospital or limited time in a skilled nursing facility

---

[30] https://www.medicare.gov/supplements-other-insurance
[31] https://www.medicare.gov/what-medicare-covers

following a hospital stay. It also pays for some home healthcare and hospice care.

I say some, because there are some deductibles you have to satisfy, and they may change every year.

Part B

Part B is medical insurance. It helps pay for services from doctors and other healthcare providers, outpatient care, home healthcare, and certain medical equipment. When you sign up, you start paying a monthly premium, which comes out of your Social Security check.

Social Security and Medicare

It's important to understand that when you take Social Security, Medicare Part A is part of that, but Part B you have to pay for and this out of pocket cost could be higher for some based on income. To get full benefits you must have paid into Social Security for 40 quarters, or 10 years of employment. If you don't have enough quarters, then you may have to pay out of pocket for Part A. Most people don't know that.

Delaying Medicare Part B

When I retired, I was under a pension plan, but also a health insurance program. I chose not to go into Medicare Part B at age 65. So when I started collecting Social Security, I did that because I had health insurance coverage. So it made no sense to switch until my full retirement age of 66.

If you are part of a qualified group plan, with 20 or more employees covered, you can stay under that, or go to Part B depending upon which one is best for you. You don't automatically join Part B when you get Part A. But it is important that when you register for part A, you let Social Security know, you are covered under a group insurance program and will be deferring Part B into the future. If you don't, you may find that you're paying for Part B, and you didn't mean to.

Part C[32]

Part C is made up of what are called Medicare Advantage plans. This is a special program established by Congress in an attempt to control healthcare costs. You sign up with a private insurer for your Advantage plan,

---

[32] https://www.hhs.gov/answers/medicare-and-medicaid/what-is-medicare-part-c/index.html

yet are still enrolled in parts A and B (including paying Part B premiums).

In Tallahassee, where I live, the city and surrounding counties have Capital Health Plan, which state employees may be members of. It's an HMO. Each region has their own providers, generally HMOs or PPOs.

Part D[33]

Part D is for prescription drugs. If you take medication regularly for a chronic condition, it's a good idea to get this plan. Keep in mind there is an open enrollment period each year, from Oct. 15 to Dec. 7, and if you miss it, you'll have to wait until the following year to join. You've probably noticed there are a lot of TV commercials about Medicare around that time of year.

How Much You'll Pay for Medicare

The government uses the IRMAA (Income Related Monthly Adjusted Amount)[34] test to determine the amount. Here's how it works. When you sign up for Medicare Part B, you'll generally pay, in 2020, $144.60 per month. However, if you earn over a certain income level, which Medicare decides each year, you could pay as much as over $500 per month.

---

[33] https://www.medicare.gov/drug-coverage-part-d
[34] https://www.medicare.gov/your-medicare-costs/part-b-costs

Your income in retirement will impact how much you pay for Medicare Part B. The government looks back two years to determine your income, which leads to some nasty surprises for some people, especially if you take a large amount of money out of your retirement accounts.

For example, I had one client who took money out of her IRA to go on trip. Two years later, her Medicare Part B payment rose significantly, and she was definitely caught by surprise.

That means when you're making decisions about an income from your retirement accounts, you must always pay attention to where you stand related to the income level thresholds Medicare has established.

Often, this sudden increase in payments is related to your required minimum distributions from your retirement accounts, which you are forced to take. This income you haven't had before could easily push you up into another bracket for the IRMAA test.

And remember that what you pay for any supplemental policy is in addition to what you pay for Part B.

The "Hidden" Cost of Medicare

In 2019, the Part B premium was $135.50, and in 2020 it was $144.60. That's a roughly $9 increase. You might say it's not that big of a deal in one year.

But if you're retired, and all you have is your pension and Social Security, because you didn't save or plan and have other resources, then that $9 increase every two or three years or every year, erodes your net income.[35]

And if you receive tax increases too, that hurts. That's why most people do not feel the effects of cost of healthcare, or inflation in general until they've been retired five to seven years, which is enough time to see the cost of living increases in your regular expenses, like going to the grocery store.

---

[35] https://www.medicare.gov/your-medicare-costs/medicare-costs-at-a-glance

Medicare Payments and
Required Minimum Distributions

I have said for years that Congress should do away with the required minimum distribution, which we talk about more in-depth in the next chapter. If you are frugal and you saved your money, you should not be forced to take it out.

Because if you have retirement resources, you're putting less pressure on the system (meaning Social Security) and they could help other people.

The reason the government insists on required minimum distributions is they want the tax money. It can be quite shocking. All these years you defer and defer, thinking you were saving taxes. But when it comes time for required minimum distribution you realize you didn't save any taxes, you simply deferred it to the future.

You do get a cost-of-living adjustment with Social Security. But soon enough, you see that disappear because the Medicare Part B premium was raised, and you have to pay for it. And then if you get impacted by IRMAA, you have a further increase. In short, the government always gets their tax dollars.

CHAPTER 7

What You May Not Know About Required Minimum Distributions

No matter what type of retirement account you have, IRA, 403(b), 457 deferred comp, SEP plan, 401(k)... the day will come when you have to start taking money. That's called a required minimum distribution.

(With Roth IRAs, you're not required to take an RMD. You may let the money sit there until the day you die. Now whoever inherits it will have to take some RMDs, but not you during your lifetime.)[36]

Many people say that they don't want the money and wonder why they're being forced to take it out at a cer-

---

[36] https://www.investopedia.com/roth-ira-required-minimum-distribution-rmd-4770561

tain age (currently, with the new Secure Act it's 72, it used to be 70 ½. And you have to take it out by April of the following year after you turn 72).[37]

Let's use a hypothetical example to see how you might approach this. Say you're 68 and in the Florida Retirement System, and you decide to retire. You've got a quarter-million dollars in your deferred compensation account. When should you take that income? You could take it immediately, or you could defer to 72.

However, the laws are very clear on this. If you have deferred compensation and, say, an IRA, you have to take distributions from both. If you have four IRAs, you may take the distribution from one, if you want to let the others continue to grow.

If you have a 403(b), 457 deferred compensation, and IRA, and you leave them in that status, you have to take money from all. That may not be the best way to do it. you may want to have some accounts giving you income today, and the others growing as long as possible. That decision comes down to when you need the money and when you're willing to pay tax on it.

---

[37] https://www.investopedia.com/secure-act-4688468

Also, how are you structuring your money? Are you primarily leaving it behind for family members? Or do you want to spend it all yourself during your lifetime?

However, the key for people in the FRS is to coordinate all savings and investments with whatever pension option they choose.

Why can't the money simply build up and then you get to pass it on to your kids?

The answer is simple.

What RMDs Really Are

RMDs were never designed to create income for you. It's a way for Congress and the IRS to recover the taxes that you didn't pay when you were accumulating that money. And they're finding more and more ways to collect the taxes... and faster too.[38]

Here's how it works in action.

Say you have $150,000 in a 403(b). At age 72, you take the value as of Dec. 31 of the previous year and, currently, you take 3.91% of that amount out of your account. By

---

[38]https://www.washingtonpost.com/business/2020/02/03/retirement-plan-rmds-secure-act/

age 80, you have to take out 5.35%. At age 85, it's 6.76%. These percentages change every year.

Let's put this into perspective. Say you've been a very conservative investor with your retirement accounts. You've parked your money in a money market fund or a bank CD earning 1% or less. If you have to take out 3.91%, you're going backward aren't you?

That means it's very important that if you have money in a retirement account that you don't get so ultra-conservative when you retire and so worried about losing money that you move it all into a low-risk money market account, which often people do. Then they get hit with the required minimum distribution, and they're seeing their account drop because they're tapping into principal at a faster pace.

There are a lot of moving parts when it comes to RMDs. You have to consider several factors:

- When do I really need the income?
- Am I going to manage it myself?
- Am I going to invest in a way that I give myself a chance to outrun the distribution requirements?
- What happens when I die? Does my spouse or children get the money or not?

No More Stretch IRAs

The Secure Act[39] did away with something called a stretch IRA.[40] That was a provision, where if you died, and did not have a surviving spouse, you leave the money to your children, and they could stretch it out over their life expectancy. So you're 50 years old, your parents died, they left you an IRA, you didn't have to take it all today and pay taxes, you could take an income based on your life expectancy.

That was a great planning tool. A lot of our clients did it because they didn't need all the money today. And they didn't want to take any but they at least took a small sliver of it.

Well, that was changed. Now, a non-spouse beneficiary who gets an inherited IRA must liquidate that account by year 10. Ten years after the account holder's death, the account must be emptied. It's just another way to collect taxes faster.

---

[39] https://www.investopedia.com/secure-act-4688468

[40] https://www.marketwatch.com/story/the-secure-act-killed-the-stretch-ira-here-are-alternatives-for-your-inheritance-2020-02-06

Considerations With Your RMDs

One of the issues I see most often with RMDs deals with people with multiple accounts. For example, I'll see someone who has an IRA, a 457 deferred compensation program with the state, and maybe a 403(b) with a previous employer. They've been told that they can just aggregate, meaning add up the total and then take the percentage from any of the accounts for their RMD.

That was true at one time – but not anymore. Now, each account stands on its own... with one exception. If you have multiple IRAs or 403(b)s, you may take the RMD from one. So currently each category stands on its own.

That means, in the case of having an IRA, 457 deferred compensation plan, and a 403(b), you must take a distribution from each category. You should consider if you need all the income from the retirement accounts or can you take the RMD from one account and let the others grow. You may always reevaluate and change the source next year based on what happens in the account.

Some of my clients will intentionally spend down one account over a 10-year period to satisfy the RMD requirement and give them more income because it gives the other accounts 10 years to grow.

As with everything we've discussed in this book, the strategy you choose should be based on your specific situation based on Social Security, pension, and other sources of income.

If people don't know that they must take an RMD, it's easy to slip up and miss it. And if you do that, you're faced with a 50% tax penalty on the amount you were supposed to take. And that's on top of the tax you have to pay.

For example, let's say your RMD is $10,000, and you don't take it. So you have to pay tax, let's call it 30%. Then you have the 50% penalty.

So don't miss it! The financial institutions make it pretty easy for you to know what your RMD is because the IRS requires that they send you a statement detailing what it is. Of course, you have to read your statements – and you'd be surprised how many people don't.

CONCLUSION

Your mindset coming into retirement is going to drive every decision you make. There are two main mindsets I see among people who come into my office seeking guidance... two ends of the spectrum.

1 People who are frustrated at work and trying to escape as soon as possible. They're sick and tired of it.

2 People who love their work and their colleagues... but they have other things in life they want to pursue, whether it's travel or volunteering or being with family.

In the first group, you have folks who are running *away* from something. In the second, they are running *to* something and embracing something new.

I think for anybody looking at retirement, it helps to understand the motivation. Which of those two groups do you fit into?

When I think about retirement and what I try to achieve for my clients, it comes down to freedom.

- Relationship freedom
- Time freedom
- Money freedom
- Location freedom

With the right retirement plan, everything you do can go through those filters. You may do the things you want, with the people you want, where you want... and you have the money to make it happen.

That's not to say that you have to travel or start volunteering. You don't have to make new friends or anything like that. If you want to simply relax and sit on the porch, that's totally up to you. The point is that you have the freedom to do whatever you want.

However, you must realize, if you plan to have an active retirement, you're probably going to need more resources to sustain that lifestyle.

Retirement is like a giant jigsaw puzzle, where they don't even give you the picture on the box to help you put the pieces together. And maybe they mix two puzzles together with pieces that don't fit. Somebody's got to somehow sort it all out and make it work.

Trying to figure out taxes, Medicare, pension plans, retirement accounts, Social Security... and all the rest, it's hard enough for experts to keep track of it all, let alone an average person. That means those seeking help with their retirement planning need to have another mindset: a willingness to suspend judgement and learn.

One of the most common misconceptions is that you need X amount of money to retire. But what's more important is that you have a monthly guaranteed income stream for life. That means $1 million in the bank or in retirement accounts might not take care of you if you don't have the right distribution plan.

What people don't realize is it's not just about the amount of money you save and invest. It's how you manage your retirement funds, your assets, pension, Social Security, healthcare costs, etc. to provide a lifetime income.

You have to consider:

How do you make this money last you for the rest of your life and your spouse's life? And then when you both die, who gets it? How do they get it? When do they get it?

When I start asking those questions, that's when people start admitting that they have no idea; they've never thought about it because they've been focused on reaching some magic number.

I created the Secure Retirement Method to take people from wherever they are now, consider their mindset and goals, and help them fund the life they want.

I developed this unique process because I was tired of reinventing the wheel every time a new client would come in. So I formalized a process for retirement planning. I focus on four steps for the people our team serves.

1. The Vision Session

You begin exploring your current situation and new possibilities for your future. This is where we determine what you have, what's working, and what's not working. We look at the good, the bad, and the ugly.

The first question I'm going to ask you is: I want you to think ahead to the day you retire, whether it's five years, 10 years, or 15 years from now, what has to happen for you to be happy in retirement? And I'll have people who say, "I have no idea."

In that case, we probably should start there. Because if you don't have some clarity on what you want to do in retirement, what I call your vision of retirement, it doesn't really matter how much money you've got and how much time you have, if you don't have any idea what to do with time and money.

I ask these folks to tell me about their interests... what they like to do. And then they'll start opening up.

2. The Discovery Session

A detailed assessment and analysis of your current financial situation and a baseline to build on.

3. The Strategy Session

We start looking for solutions based on our initial conversations. It's a step-by-step planning process to develop strategies, choose tools, and build a team to achieve your goals.

4. The Implementation Session

You've got to take action. (If you don't have a will, you need to get one drafted. If you need a certain financial product, you need to invest in it.) This is a system of tools, resources, capabilities, and expertise for effectively implementing your plans.

At the end of step 3, you will have a written document that lays it all out for you; a clear path to a fulfilling retirement specific to your needs and wants.

There are four things you may do with this data:

- Ignore it
- Do it by yourself
- Go to another financial advisor
- Work with my team on implementation

You're free to do whatever you want.

I'm not interested in working with people who simply want to buy a certain product they've heard about, like a mutual fund or life insurance plan. Because I feel it's vital to understand your financial picture and help you make decisions based on that.

You don't really need me, you can do it yourself, if that's what you want to do. To be honest, I only want to attract people who know they need help. They want help. And they want to be a partner in that I'm not doing it all for you by myself, you're going to be engaged in the process.

We work together, although you'll ultimately have to make the decisions. But I can coach you and guide you and make sure that you're on the right path.

I've been helping folks do that very thing with their financial and retirement planning since 1975. Along the way, I've collected a bunch of letters behind my name:

- CLU – Chartered Life Underwriter
- ChFC - Chartered Financial Consultant
- AEP – Accredited Estate Planner
- MSFS – Master of Science in Financial Services
- CLTC – Certified Long-Term Care

But I think what sets me apart is the experience, knowledge, and expertise I've picked up over the last 45+ years.

If we work together, it all starts with a phone call to get to know each other.

Then you go through my Secure Retirement Method process outlined above, if you like what you see.

Then I like to do what I call a retirement rehearsal for my clients. We take every stream of income you have, we put it into our model, we project you out to age 100, and see how it works with various retirement accounts and planning decisions.

To get started, call the office at 850-562-3000 and one of my team members will help you schedule a 20-minute introductory call.

Retirement Planning Course Exclusively for Members of The Florida Retirement System

Here's what you'll discover in this complimentary course:

- FRS Pension Options - What are the four options and how do they work?
- Retirement Accounts - Your options for your 457 Deferred Compensation plans, DROP, 403(b), IRAs and other retirement accounts.
- Social Security - All your Social Security questions answered (plus the ones you didn't even know to ask).
- Medicare - How to navigate the complex topic of Medicare.
- Required Minimum Distributions - What are RMDs? How will they impact your retirement?

info.johnhcurry.com/frs-course

The Secure Retirement Podcast

Listen as John discusses key issues for anyone nearing or in retirement and interviews retirees who are living their Secure Retirement.

johnhcurry.com/podcast

Regular Webinars on Important Retirement Topics

Join John and his team for monthly webinars on a range of topics including: The Florida Retirement System, Social Security, Medicare, The 7 Mistakes Most People Make When Planning for a Secure Retirement, and more.

johnhcurry.com/webinar

The Secure Retirement Scorecard

Take the Secure Retirement Scorecard and see where you stand in 10 the key areas. In less than 5 minutes you'll have a sense of where you stand now, and which issues are most important to address next. The scorecard may be found on Page 8 of this book, or you may download a printable copy online.

johnhcurry.com/scorecard

Dear Friend,

Thank you for sharing your time with me as you read this book.

I am a passionate advocate of protecting families and their futures through what I do. That's why I am writing this note inviting you to come in for a No cost, No Obligation FOCUS Session.

In the FOCUS Session we will talk about:

Your Future
Your Opportunities
Your Concerns
Your Uniqueness
Your Strengths

At the end of our 45-minute session we will both know if it makes sense for us to meet again. If yes, we'll schedule another appointment. If no, we'll part having had the benefit of clarifying your goals and future. A win for everyone, with NO RISK to you!

John

P.S. This session can also be conducted by phone/computer conference.

Made in the USA
Columbia, SC
14 March 2021

34495239R00052